SandCastle 3

Homonyms

A Palm in My Palm

Kelly Doudna

ABDO Publishing Company

Published by SandCastle™, an imprint of ABDO Publishing Company, 4940 Viking Drive, Edina, Minnesota 55435.

Printed in the United States.

Photo credits: Artville, Corbis Images, Digital Vision, Eyewire Images, PhotoDisc, Rubberball Productions

Library of Congress Cataloging-in-Publication Data

Doudna, Kelly, 1963-
    A palm in my palm / Kelly Doudna.
        p. cm. -- (Homonyms)
    Includes index.
    Summary: Photographs and simple text introduce homonyms, words that are spelled and sound the same but have different meanings.
    ISBN 1-57765-790-X
        1. English language--Homonyms--Juvenile literature. [1. English language--Homonyms.] I. Title.

PE1595 .D76 2002
428.1--dc21

2001053323

The SandCastle concept, content, and reading method have been reviewed and approved by a national advisory board including literacy specialists, librarians, elementary school teachers, early childhood education professionals, and parents.

Let Us Know

After reading the book, SandCastle would like you to tell us your stories about reading. What is your favorite page? Was there something hard that you needed help with? Share the ups and downs of learning to read. We want to hear from you! To get posted on the Abdo Publishing Company Web site, send us email at:

sandcastle@abdopub.com

About SandCastle™

Nonfiction books for the beginning reader

- Basic concepts of phonics are incorporated with integrated language methods of reading instruction. Most words are short, and phrases, letter sounds, and word sounds are repeated.

- Book levels are based on the ATOS™ for Books formula. Other considerations for readability include the number of words in each sentence, the number of characters in each word, and word lists based on curriculum frameworks.

- Full-color photography reinforces word meanings and concepts.

- "Words I Can Read" list at the end of each book teaches basic elements of grammar, helps the reader recognize the words in the text, and builds vocabulary.

- Reading levels are indicated by the number of flags on the castle.

SandCastle uses the following definitions for this series:

- Homographs: words that are spelled the same but sound different and have different meanings. *Easy memory tip: "-graph"= same look*

- Homonyms: words that are spelled and sound the same but have different meanings. *Easy memory tip: "-nym"= same name*

- Homophones: words that sound alike but are spelled differently and have different meanings. *Easy memory tip: "-phone"= sound alike*

Look for more SandCastle books in these three reading levels:

Level 1 (one flag)	**Level 2** (two flags)	**Level 3** (three flags)

Grades Pre-K to K 5 or fewer words per page	**Grades K to 1** 5 to 10 words per page	**Grades 1 to 2** 10 to 15 words per page

pitcher

pitcher

Homonyms are words that are spelled and sound the same but have different meanings.

I dress like a nurse.

I have a part in the school play.

I comb my hair every morning.
I part it on the right side.

This pig lives on a farm.

It is kept in a pen.

I study at school.

I write in my notebook with a pen.

I have a rabbit named Henry.

He is my pet.

I pet my rat.

I know she likes to be stroked gently.

I am doing a lesson on the computer.

I point to the correct answer.

I like to write stories.

My pencil has a sharp point.

I want to earn money.

I will post a sign to get work.

The signs on the post say we are at the corner of Main and School Streets.

A prune is a dried plum.

Prunes provide iron for our bodies.

Mom has a garden.

She will prune the flowers to help them grow.

We see with our eyes.

The black circle in the center is the pupil.

Ms. Miller is my teacher.

I am a pupil in her class.

I arrived at school on time.

I am present for roll call.

My birthday happens once a year.

What will I unwrap?

(present)

Words I Can Read
Nouns

A noun is a person, place, or thing

answer (AN-sur) p. 12
birthday (BURTH-day)
  p. 21
bodies (BOD-eez) p. 16
center (SEN-tur) p. 18
circle (SUR-kuhl) p. 18
class (KLASS) p. 19
computer
  (kuhm-PYOO-tur)
  p. 12
corner (KOR-nur) p. 15
eyes (EYEZ) p. 18
farm (FARM) p. 8
flowers (FLOU-urz)
  p. 17
garden (GARD-uhn)
  p. 17
hair (HAIR) p. 7
homonyms
  (HOM-uh-nimz) p. 5
iron (EYE-urn) p. 16
lesson (LESS-uhn) p. 12

meanings (MEE-ningz)
  p. 5
money (MUHN-ee) p. 14
morning (MOR-ning)
  p. 7
notebook (NOHT-buk)
  p. 9
nurse (NURSS) p. 6
part (PART) p. 6
pen (PEN) pp. 8, 9
pencil (PEN-suhl) p. 13
pet (PET) p. 10
pig (PIG) p. 8
pitcher (PICH-ur) p. 4
plum (PLUHM) p. 16
point (POINT) p. 13
post (POHST) p. 15
present (PREZ-uhnt)
  p. 21
prune (PROON)
  p. 16

prunes (PROONZ)
  p. 16
pupil (PYOO-puhl)
  pp. 18, 19
rabbit (RAB-it) p. 10
rat (RAT) p. 11
roll call (ROHL KAWL)
  p. 20
school (SKOOL)
  pp. 9, 20
school play
  (SKOOL PLAY) p. 6
side (SIDE) p. 7
sign (SINE) p. 14
signs (SINEZ) p. 15
stories (STOR-eez) p. 13
teacher (TEECH-ur)
  p. 19
time (TIME) p. 20
words (WURDZ) p. 5
work (WURK) p. 14
year (YIHR) p. 21

Proper Nouns

A proper noun is the name of a
person, place, or thing

Henry (HEN-ree) p. 10
Main Street
  (MAYN STREET) p. 15

Mom (MOM) p. 17
Ms. Miller
  (MIZ MIL-ur) p. 19

School Street
  (SKOOL STREET) p. 15

Pronouns

A pronoun is a word that replaces a noun

he (HEE) p. 10

I (EYE) pp. 6, 7, 9, 10, 11, 12, 13, 14, 18, 19, 20, 21

it (IT) pp. 7, 8

she (SHEE) pp. 11, 17

that (THAT) p. 5

them (THEM) p. 17

we (WEE) p. 15

what (WUHT) p. 21

Verbs

A verb is an action or being word

am (AM) pp. 12, 19, 20

are (AR) pp. 5, 15

arrived (uh-RIVED) p. 20

be (BEE) p. 11

comb (KOHM) p. 7

doing (DOO-ing) p. 12

dress (DRESS) p. 6

earn (URN) p. 14

get (GET) p. 14

grow (GROH) p. 17

happens (HAP-uhnz) p. 21

has (HAZ) pp. 13, 17

have (HAV) pp. 5, 6, 10

help (HELP) p. 17

is (IZ) pp. 8, 10, 16, 18, 19

kept (KEPT) p. 8

know (NOH) p. 11

like (LIKE) p. 13

likes (LIKESS) p. 11

lives (LIVZ) p. 8

named (NAYMD) p. 10

part (PART) p. 7

pet (PET) p. 11

point (POINT) p. 12

post (POHST) p. 14

provide (pruh-VIDE) p. 16

prune (PROON) p. 17

say (SAY) p. 15

see (SEE) p. 18

sound (SOUND) p. 5

spelled (SPELD) p. 5

stroked (STROHKT) p. 11

study (STUHD-ee) p. 9

unwrap (uhn-RAP) p. 21

want (WONT) p. 14

will (WIL) pp. 14, 17, 21

write (RITE) pp. 9, 13

Adjectives

An adjective describes something

black (BLAK) p. 18
correct (kuh-REKT) p. 12
different (DIF-ur-uhnt) p. 5
dried (DRYED) p. 16

every (EV-ree) p. 7
her (HUR) p. 19
my (MYE) pp. 7, 9, 10, 11, 13, 18, 19, 21
our (OUR) p. 16

present (PREZ-uhnt) p. 20
right (RITE) p. 7
same (SAYM) p. 5
sharp (SHARP) p. 13
this (THISS) p. 8

Adverbs

An adverb tells how, when, or where something happens

gently (JENT-lee) p. 11   once (WUHNSS) p. 21